The Nature and Purpose of the Church

A stage on the way to a common statement

Faith and Order Paper No. 181

November 1998

Cover design: Edwin Hassink

© WCC/Faith and Order
   150 Route de Ferney
   1211 Geneva 2
   Switzerland

ISBN 2-8254-1302-X

Printed in November 1998
by Orthdruk Orthodox Printing House, Bialystok, Poland

Contents

INTRODUCTION

Background

1.   Since its beginning, and especially at the First World Conference, Lausanne, Switzerland, 1927, the Faith and Order Movement identified the unity of the Church as the very reason for its existence. Thus the By-Laws of the Faith and Order Commission state that its aim is:

> to proclaim the oneness of the Church of Jesus Christ and to call the churches to the goal of visible unity in one faith and one eucharistic fellowship, expressed in worship and in common life in Christ, in order that the world may believe.

Since Amsterdam, 1948, this goal has been at the heart of the common calling of the World Council of Churches itself. Moreover, in all the Assemblies of the World Council of Churches, the particular contribution of Faith and Order has been to deepen a common understanding of this goal and of the ways to realise it. The most recent contribution is focused in the statement of the Canberra Assembly – "The Church as *Koinonia*: Gift and Calling". The statement shows that *koinonia* is both the foundation and the way of living a life together in visible unity. This was echoed in the theme of the Fifth World Conference on Faith and Order, Towards *Koinonia* in Faith, Life and Witness. The present process on Towards a Common Understanding and Vision of the WCC again underlines the common calling of the churches as the search for visible unity.

2.   All the major documents issued by Faith and Order contribute in some way or other to the understanding of the nature and purpose of the Church. Moreover, *Baptism, Eucharist and Ministry, Confessing the One Faith* and *Church and World,* sent to the churches for response and

reception, are ways of keeping alive in the churches the imperative of Christ's call to visible unity and the essential characteristics of that unity. In the last decade work on ecclesiology and ethics, which continued the studies on, for example, racism and the community of women and men in the Church, has contributed to the understanding of our common Christian calling in the service of humanity and creation. In its turn Faith and Order receives constantly insights about the unity to which God calls us from responses of the churches to its studies, the results of the bilateral dialogues, the work in other areas of the World Council of Churches and from reflection on the experience of the United and Uniting Churches.

This Study

3.   A study on the nature and purpose of the Church was strongly recommended by the Fifth World Conference on Faith and Order in Santiago de Compostela, Spain (1993). This was a timely call for many reasons:

- ° the time is right for Faith and Order to reflect on the different insights which its own studies offer to an understanding of the nature and purpose of the Church;

- ° the opportunity is there for Faith and Order to draw upon the fruits of the work of other parts of the WCC and of the bilateral theological agreements;

- ° growth in fellowship is being experienced between Christians at local, national and world levels, not least of all in the experience of united and uniting churches;

- ° particular challenges in many regions call out for Christians together to address what it means to be Church in that place;

- ° the situation of the world demands and deserves a credible witness to unity in diversity which is God's gift for the whole of humanity.

Purpose and Method

4.   The main purpose of this study is to give expression to what the churches can now say together about the nature and purpose of the Church and within that perspective to state the remaining areas of disagreement. Thus, in the style of *BEM*, this document seeks to evolve into what could be called a convergence text. The present text is a first attempt to state that convergence. It is offered for study and discernment.

5.   The **main text** represents common perspectives which can be claimed largely as a result of the work of the bilateral and multilateral discussions of the past fifty years. The **material inside the boxes** explores areas where differences remain both within and between churches. Some of these differences may come to be seen as expressions of legitimate diversity, others as church-dividing. While the main text invites the churches to discover or rediscover how much they in fact have in common in their understanding of the Church, the text in the boxes offers the opportunity for churches to reflect on the extent to which their divergences are church-dividing. In the perspective of growing convergences, the hope is that churches will be helped to recognise in one another the Church of Jesus Christ and be encouraged to take steps on the way towards visible unity.

6.   Any ecumenical document raises the question of how Scripture is used. The agreements of this text are based upon a common understanding of the unique and normative revelation of the Scripture and thus the need to ground our agreement in the witness of Holy Scripture. At the same time it is recognised that in the Holy Scripture there is no systematic ecclesiology. The theme of the Church is largely presented through a variety of images which interact and complement each other. The approach of the present text is to take Scripture as a whole, in such a way that one part of Scripture interprets the other and is interpreted by the others.*

---

* Response to a preliminary distibution of the present text has indicated dissatisfaction with the approach to Scripture described in this paragraph. More work is clearly required in the next stages towards a convergence text, in the way in which Scripture is cited and interpreted.

The Invitation

7.   The Faith and Order Commission invites churches, commissions, colleges, institutes, and individuals to reflect on the text in the light of the following questions:

- ° how far can you recognize in this text an emerging convergence on the nature and purpose of the Church?
- ° what areas in particular do you consider need further work and what insights can you offer to progress that work?
- ° what other areas need to be treated in a convergence document on the nature and purpose of the Church?
- ° if you can recognize in this text an emerging convergence on the nature and purpose of the Church, what implications has this for your relation with other churches who may also recognize that convergence? What steps might your churches take even now towards mutual recognition?

Responses will be essential as Faith and Order continues its work to develop a common agreed statement on the nature and purpose of the Church.

8.   In God's design the Church exists, not for itself alone, but to serve in God's work of reconciliation and for the praise and glory of God. The more the Church understands its own nature, the more it gets hold of its own vocation. Hence the crucial importance of this study on the nature and the purpose of the Church.

I.   THE CHURCH OF THE TRIUNE GOD

A.   The Nature of the Church

(i)   The Church as Creation of the Word and of the Holy Spirit (*creatura Verbi et creatura Spiritus*)

9.   The Church belongs to God. It is the creation of God's Word and Holy Spirit. It cannot exist by and for itself.

10.   The Church is centred and grounded in the Gospel, the Word of God. The Church is the communion of those who live in a personal relationship with God who speaks to them and calls forth their trustful response – the communion of the faithful. Thus the Church is the creature of God's Word which as a living voice creates and nourishes it throughout the ages. This divine Word is borne witness to and makes itself heard through the scriptures. Incarnate in Jesus Christ, it is testified to by the Church and proclaimed in preaching, in sacraments, and in service.

11.   Faith called forth by the Word of God is brought about by the action of the Holy Spirit. In the scriptures, the Word of God and the Holy Spirit are inseparable. As the communion of the faithful, the Church therefore is also the creation of the Holy Spirit (*creatura Spiritus*). As in the life of Christ the Holy Spirit was active from the conception to the resurrection, so also in the life of the Church the same Spirit of God forms Christ in all believers and their community. The Spirit incorporates human beings into the body of Christ through faith and baptism, enlivens and strengthens them as the body of Christ nourished and sustained at the Lord's Supper, and leads them to the full accomplishment of their vocation.

12.   Being the creature of God's own Word and Spirit the Church of God is one, holy, catholic and apostolic. These essential attributes of

the Church are not its own qualities but are fully rooted in its dependence upon God through his Word and Spirit. It is **one** because the God who binds it to himself by Word and Spirit is the one creator and redeemer making the Church a foretaste and instrument for the redemption of all created reality. It is **holy** because God is the holy one who in Jesus Christ has overcome all unholiness, sanctifying the Church by his word of forgiveness in the Holy Spirit and making it his own, the body of Christ. It is **catholic** because God is the fulness of life who through Word and Spirit makes the Church the place and instrument of his saving, life-giving, fulfilling presence wherever it is, thereby offering the fullness of the revealed Word, all the means of salvation to people of every nation, race, class, sex and culture. It is **apostolic** because the Word of God that creates and sustains the Church is the Gospel primarily and normatively borne witness to by the apostles, making the communion of the faithful a community that lives in, and is responsible for, the succession of the apostolic truth throughout the ages.

13.   The Church is not the sum of individual believers in communion with God. It is not primarily a communion of believers with each other. It is their common partaking in God's own life whose innermost being is communion. Thus it is a divine and human reality.

The Institutional Dimension of the Church and the Work of the Holy Spirit

All churches agree that God creates the Church and binds it to himself through the Holy Spirit by means of the living voice of the Gospel proclaimed in preaching and in the sacraments. Yet they have different opinions as to:

(1) whether the preaching and the sacraments are the means of, or simply witnesses to, the activity of the Spirit through the divine Word which comes about in an immediate internal action upon the hearts of the believers;

(2) the institutional implications and presuppositions of the Church's being creatura Verbi: for some the ordained ministry, particularly episcopacy, is the effective means, for some even the guarantee of the presence of truth and power of the Word and Spirit of God in the Church; for others the fact that the ordained ministry as well as the witness of all believers are subject to error and sin excludes such a judgment, the power and reliability of God's truth being grounded in the sovereignty of his Word and Spirit which works through, but if necessary also counter to, the given institutional structures of the Church;

(3) the theological importance of institutional continuity, particularly continuity in episcopacy: whereas for some churches such institutional continuity is the necessary means and guarantee of the Church's continuity in apostolic faith, for others continuity in apostolic faith under certain circumstances is being kept in spite of, and even through, the break of institutional continuity. It remains for future theological work to find out whether these differences are real disagreements or mere differences in emphasis that can be reconciled with each other.

(ii)   Images of the Church

14.   The Almighty God, who calls the Church into being and unites it to himself through his Word and the Holy Spirit, is the Triune God, Father, Son and Holy Spirit. In its relationship to God the Church is related to each of these divine "Persons" in a particular way. These particular relations signify different dimensions of the Church's life.

15.   In the Holy Scripture there is no systematic ecclesiology. The theme of the Church is largely dealt with by way of various images. Some are images of stability and locality, some of mobility, some are more organic images, some stress the relational character of the Church. These are not mutually exclusive. They interact, and quite often they support and comment on each other's weaker and stronger aspects. The approach of the present text in dealing with these images is to take the Scriptures as a whole, in such a way that no image is taken as an isolated point of reference, but each interprets the other and is interpreted by the others (cf. note at para. 6 above).

16.   Among scriptural images of the Church, some became particularly prominent, referring to the Trinitarian dimensions of the Church. Among these, the images of the "people of God" and the "body of Christ" are particularly important, accompanied by the imagery of "temple" or "house" of the Spirit. It must be noted, however, that none of these images is exclusive but all of them implicitly or explicitly include the other Trinitarian dimensions as well.

(a)   Church as People of God

17.   In the calling of Abraham, God was choosing for himself a holy people. The recalling of this election and vocation found frequent expression in the words of the prophets: "I will be their God and they shall be my people" (Jer 31:33; Ez 37:27; Hos 2:23, echoed in 2 Cor 6:16; Heb 8:10). Through the Word (*dabhar*) of God and the Spirit (*rû'ah*) of God, God chose and formed one from among the nations to bring salvation to all. The election of Israel marked a decisive moment

in the realization of the plan of salvation. This covenant entails many things, including a calling to justice and truth. But it is also a gracious gift of *koinonia,* a dynamic impulse to communion which is evident throughout the story of the people of Israel, even when the community breaks *koinonia.* In the light of the ministry, teaching, and above all the death and resurrection of Jesus and the sending of the Holy Spirit at Pentecost, the Christian community believes that God sent his Son to bring the possibility of communion for each person with others and with God, thus manifesting the gift of God for the whole world.

18.   In the Old Testament, the people of Israel is a pilgrim people journeying towards the fulfilment of the promise that in Abraham all the nations of the earth shall be blessed. In Christ this is fulfilled when, on the cross, the dividing wall between Jew and Gentile is broken down (Eph 2:14). Thus the Church, embracing Jew and Gentile is a "chosen race, a royal priesthood, a holy nation", "God's own people" (1 Peter 2:9-10). The Church of God continues the way of pilgrimage to the eternal rest prepared for it (Heb 4:9-11). It is a prophetic sign of the fulfilment God will bring about through Christ by the power of the Spirit.

(b)   Church as Body of Christ

19.   Through the blood of Christ, God's purpose was to reconcile humanity in one body through the cross (Eph 2:11-22). This body is the body of Christ, the Church (Eph 1:23). Christ is the abiding head of this body and at the same time the one who, by the presence of the Spirit, gives life to it. In this way, Christ who is head of his body, empowering, leading and judging it (Eph 5:23; Col 1:18), is also one with his body (1 Cor 12:12; Rom 12:5). The image of the Body of Christ in the New Testament includes these two dimensions, one expressed in 1 Corinthians and Romans, the other developed in Ephesians.

20.   It is through faith and baptism that human beings become members of the body of Christ (1 Cor 12:13). Through Holy Communion their participation and communion in this body is renewed again and

again (1 Cor 10:16). Being thus members of his body, Christians identify with the unique priesthood of Christ (Heb 9), and are called to live as faithful members: "You are the holy priesthood" (1 Peter 2:9). In Christ who offered himself, Christians offer their whole being "as a living sacrifice" (Rom 12:1). Every member participates in the priesthood of the whole Church. No one exercises that priesthood apart from the unique priesthood of Christ, nor in isolation from the other members of the body.

21.   All members of Christ are given gifts for the building up of the body (Rom 12:4-8; 1 Cor 12:4-30), the diversity and specific nature of which serve the Church's own life and its vocation as servant, for the furthering of God's kingdom in the world.

22.   According to the New Testament, it is through the Holy Spirit that human beings are baptized into the body of Christ (1 Cor 12:13). It is the same Holy Spirit who confers the manifold gifts to the members of the body (1 Cor 12:4, 7-11) and brings forth their unity (1 Cor 12). Thus the image of "body of Christ", though explicitly and primarily referring to the christological dimension of the Church, at the same time has deep pneumatological implications.

(c)   Church as Temple of the Holy Spirit

23.   Reference to the constitutive relation between Church and Holy Spirit runs through the whole New Testament witness. Nevertheless there is no explicit image for this relation. The imagery that comes particularly close to the figurative descriptions of this relation entailed in the New Testament, and renders it in a particularly appropriate way, is the imagery of "temple" and "house". This is so because the relation of the Spirit to the Church is one of indwelling, of giving life from within.

24.   Built on the foundation of the apostles and prophets the Church is God's household, a holy temple in which God lives by the Spirit. By the power of the Holy Spirit believers grow into "a holy temple in the Lord" (Eph 2:21), into a "spiritual house" (1 Peter 2:5). Filled with the

Holy Spirit, they pray, love, work and serve in the power of the Spirit, leading a life worthy of their calling, eager to maintain the unity of the Spirit in the bond of peace (Eph 4:1-3).

25.   These three images have been chosen because of their central importance in the New Testament and because of their significance for the Trinitarian dimensions of the Church. Yet it should be mentioned that there are other images of the Church in the New Testament – most of them christological – like vine, flock, wedding party, bride. They all serve to highlight certain aspects of the Church's being and life: the vine-image stresses its total dependence on Christ, the flock-image stresses its trust and obedience, the party-image stresses the eschatological reality of the Church, the bride-image stresses the intimate though subordinate relation of the Church to Christ. At the same time these images – like all images, also those listed in (a) to (c) – have their limits: the vine image does not take into account the vis-à-vis relation between Christ and the Church; the flock-image does not take into account the freedom of the believers; the party image does not take into account the not-yet-fulfilled dimension of the Church's life *in via;* the bride-image presupposes the subordinate status of women in ancient times.

B.   God's Purpose for the Church

26.   It is God's design to gather all creation under the Lordship of Christ (Eph 1:10), and to bring humanity and all creation into communion. As a reflection of the communion in the Triune God, the Church is called by God to be the instrument in fulfilling this goal. The Church is called to manifest God's mercifulness to humanity, and to restore humanity's natural purpose – to praise and glorify God together with all the heavenly hosts. As such it is not an end in itself, but a gift given to the world in order that all may believe (John 17:21).

27.   Mission belongs to the very being of the Church. As persons who acknowledge Jesus Christ as Lord and Saviour, Christians are called to proclaim the Gospel in word and deed. They are to address those who have not heard as well as to those who are no longer in living contact with the Gospel, the Good News of the reign of God. They are called to

live its values and to be a foretaste of that reign in the world.

28.   Thus the Church, embodying in its own life the mystery of salvation and the transfiguration of humanity, participates in the mission of Christ to reconcile all things to God and to one another through Christ. Through its ministry of service and proclamation and its stewardship of creation, the Church participates in and points to the reality of the Kingdom of God. In the power of the Holy Spirit, the Church testifies to the divine mission in which the Father sent the Son to be the Saviour of the world.

29.   In exercising its mission, the Church cannot be the Church without giving witness (*martyria*) to God's will for the salvation and transformation of the world. That is why it started at once preaching the Word and bearing witness to the great deeds of God and inviting everyone to baptism.

30.   As Christ's mission encompassed the preaching of the Word of God and the commitment to care for those suffering and in need, thus the apostolic Church in its mission from the beginning combined preaching of the Word, the call to baptism and service. This the Church understands as an essential dimension of its identity. The Church in this way signifies, participates in, and anticipates the new humanity God wants, and also serves to proclaim God's grace in human situations and needs until Christ comes in glory (Mt 25:31).

31.   Because the servanthood of Christ entails suffering, it is evident, as expressed in the New Testament writings, that the *martyria* of the Church will entail, for individuals and for the community, the way of the cross.

32.   The Church is called and empowered to share the suffering of all by advocacy and care for the poor, needy and marginalised. It does this by critically analysing and exposing unjust structures and by working for their transformation. It does this by its works of compassion and mercy. Thus the Church is called to heal and reconcile broken human

relationships. The Church is to be God's instrument in the eradication of enmity, the reconciliation of human division and hatred, which is the main source of human suffering. It is also called, together with all people of goodwill, to care for the integrity of creation in condemning as sinful the abuse and destruction of God's creation, and to participate in God's healing of broken relationships between creation and humanity.

33. In the power of the Holy Spirit, the Church is called to proclaim faithfully the whole teaching of Christ and to share the totality of apostolic faith, life and witness with everyone throughout the entire world. Thus, the Church seeks faithfully to proclaim and live the love of God for all, and fulfil Christ's mission for the salvation and transformation of the world to the glory of God.

34. God restores and enriches communion with humanity, granting eternal life in God's Triune being. Through humanity, the whole world is meant to be drawn to the goal of restoration and salvation. This divine plan reaches its fulfilment in the new heaven and the new earth (Rev 21:1) in God's holy Kingdom.

II.   THE CHURCH IN HISTORY

A.   The Church *in via*

35.   The Church is an eschatological reality, already anticipating the Kingdom. The Church is also a historical reality, exposed to the ambiguity of all human history and thus not yet the community God desires.

36.   On the one hand, the Church is that part of humanity which already participates in the communion of God, in faith, hope, and glorification of God's name, and lives as a communion of redeemed persons. Because of the presence of the eschatological Spirit and of the Word of God, the Church – as *creatura Verbi* and *Spiritus* (cf. paras 9ff.), as the communion of all believers held in personal relationship with God by God himself (cf. para. 10), as the people of God (cf. paras 17-18), as the body of Christ (cf. paras 19-22), as the temple of the Holy Spirit (cf. paras 23-24) – is already the eschatological community God wills.

37.   Yet at the same time the Church in its human dimension, insofar as it is made up of human beings who though being members of the body of Christ are still subject to the conditions of this world, is itself affected by these conditions. It is exposed to change, which allows for both positive development and growth as well as for the negative possibility of decline and distortion. It is exposed to individual, cultural and historical conditioning which can contribute to a richness of insights and expressions of faith but also to relativizing tendencies or absolutizing particular views. It is exposed to the Holy Spirit's free use of its power (Jn 3:8) in illuminating hearts and binding consciences. It is exposed to the power of sin.

38.   The **oneness** which belongs to the very nature of the Church and is already given to it in Jesus Christ stands in contrast to the actual divisions between the churches. These divisions, which are partly due to sin, but also due to the dilemma inherent in history that in certain

situations the integrity of truth may be upheld only in contradiction to other positions, are an anomalous fact. The churches have to strive to overcome them. Yet in spite of all divisions the unity given to the Church is already manifest in the Gospel present in all churches and appears in many features of their lives. Working for the unity of the Church means working for fuller visible embodiment of the oneness already given to it.

39. The essential **holiness** of the Church stands in contrast to sin, individual as well as communal, which in the course of the Church's history again and again has disfigured its witness and run counter to its true nature and vocation. Therefore in the Church there has been again and again God's ever new offer of forgiveness together with the call for repentance, renewal and reform. Responding to this call means fuller visible embodiment of the holiness that belongs to its nature and is already given to it.

40. The essential **catholicity** of the Church is confronted with a fragmentation of its life, a contradictory preaching of the truth. The consequence is that the integrity of the Gospel is not adequately preached to all; the wholeness of the divine means of salvation is not available to all; the fullness of communion is not offered to all; the Gospel is not received the same way in "all the nations". Nevertheless, the Spirit it receives at baptism is the Spirit of the Lordship of Christ over all creation and all times. The Church is called to remove all obstacles to the full development of what it already is by the power of the Holy Spirit.

41. The essential **apostolicity** of the Church stands in contrast to shortcomings and errors of the churches in their proclamation of the Word of God. Hence the churches are called to return continuously to the apostolic truth and to their apostolic origin. By doing so they make visible and do justice to the apostolic Gospel which is already given to them and at work in them in the Spirit and which makes them Church.

The Church and Sin

All churches agree that there is sin – individual as well as corporate – in the Church's history. They also agree that sin cannot affect the Church as a divine reality, whereas sin can affect the human reality and structures of the Church. Yet they differ in where they see the Church's divine reality, and thus in their understanding of the way the Church is affected by sin.

For some it is impossible to say "the Church sins" because they see the Church as a gift of God, and as such marked by God's holiness. The Church is the spotless Bride of Christ (Eph 5:25-27); it is the children of God who received God's incarnate Word through faith; it is the Holy People of God, "justified by the faith of Christ"; as such, the Church cannot sin, "lest Christ be the minister of sin" (Gal 2:17). This gift of the Church is lived out in fragile human beings who are liable to sin, but the sin of the members of the Church are not sins of the Church. The Church is rather the locus of salvation and healing, and not the subject of sin.

Others, while they too state that the Church as the creature of God's Word and Spirit, the body of Christ, etc., is holy and without sin, at the same time say that it does sin, because they define the Church as the communion of its members, who at the same time as being believers created by the Spirit and Christ's own body, in this world are still sinful beings.

Thus some hold that one cannot speak of the sin of the Church, but one can and must speak of the sin of the members and groups within the Church, a situation described by the parable of the wheat and the chaff, and by the Augustinian formula of corpus permixtum. *For others, sin in the Church can become systemic and also affect the institution. Some teach that it is impossible to single out individual points and items in the Church's life which can be affected by sin and others which cannot,*

> *but that this problem can only be tackled in a dialectical way: the Church itself is sinful insofar as it is a communion of those who although sanctified by God are never without sin, but it is holy insofar as it is called into being and kept in communion with God through his holy Word and the Holy Spirit.*

B.   Sign and Instrument of God's Design

42.   The one, holy, catholic and apostolic Church is the sign and instrument of God's design for the whole world. Being that part of humanity which already participates in the love and communion of God the Church is a prophetic sign which points beyond itself to the purpose of all creation, the fulfilment of the kingdom of God.

43.   Aware of God's saving presence in the world, the Church already praises and glorifies the Triune God through its worship and its discipleship and serves God's design. Yet the Church does so not only for itself, but it renders praise and thanks for God's grace and the forgiveness of sins on behalf of all creatures, and it serves God's design for the sake of all creation.

44.   To speak of the Church as sign also entails the dimension of *"mysterion"*, indicating the transcendence of its God-given reality as the one, holy, catholic and apostolic Church which can never be clearly and unequivocally grasped in its visible appearance. Therefore the visible organizational structures of the Church must always be seen in the light of God's gifts of salvation in Christ.

45.   Being that part of humanity which already participates in the love and communion of God, at the same time the Church is the instrument through which God wants to bring about what is signified by it: the salvation of the whole world, the renewal of the human community by

the divine Word and the Holy Spirit, the communion of humanity
with God and within itself.

46.   As instrument of God's design the Church is the community of
people called by God and sent as Christ's disciples to proclaim the Good
News in word and deed that the world may believe. Thus it makes
present throughout history the mercifulness of God.

47.   Sent as his disciples the people of God has to witness to and
participate in God's reconciliation, healing, and transformation of
creation. The Church's relation to Christ entails that faith and community require discipleship. The integrity of the mission of the
Church, of its very being as God's instrument therefore is at stake in
witness through proclamation and concrete actions with all people
of goodwill for justice, peace, and integrity of creation.

Church and "Sacrament"

The reality of the Church as sign and instrument of God's design is summed up by several churches in the expression: the Church as sacrament.

Those churches who use the formula "Church as sacrament" do so because they see the Church primarily as a pointer to what God wants for the world, namely the communion of all together and with him, the happiness for which he created the world.

Other churches do not apply the concept of sacrament to the Church, giving the following two main reasons: (a) there should be a clear distinction between Church and sacraments. The latter are means of salvation through which Christ sustains the Church, not actions by which the Church realizes or actualizes itself; and (b) using the term "sacrament" for the Church might obscure the fact that, for them, the Church is sign and instrument of God's design as the communion of Christians who, though being redeemed believers, are still liable to sin.

Over and above the different approaches to the "Church as sacrament" expression, there are differing views on what sacraments are in the first place. For some of the churches, sacraments are the "visible sign of the invisible grace of God". They are "effective signs" which signify and convey the grace of God. They are signs of God's promise. For others, "sacraments" are the opportunity for God's grace, utilized by God as an occasion to give his grace.

III. THE CHURCH AS *KOINONIA* (COMMUNION)

A. Communion, real but not fully realized

48. The notion of *koinonia* (communion) has become fundamental for revitalizing a common understanding of the nature of the Church and its visible unity. The term *koinonia* (communion, participation) is used in the New Testament, patristic and Reformation writings in relation to the Church. Although in later centuries the term remained in use, it is being reclaimed today in the ecumenical movement as a key to understanding the nature and the purpose of the Church. Due to its richness of meaning, it is also a convenient notion for assessing the degree of communion in various forms already achieved among Christians within the ecumenical movement.

49. The relationship between God and humanity and the whole of creation is a fundamental theme of Holy Scripture. In the narrative of creation, man and woman are created in God's image, bearing an inherent longing and capacity for communion with God, with one another and with creation as its stewards. Thus, the whole of creation has its integrity in *koinonia* with God. Communion is rooted in the order of creation itself, and is realized in part in natural relationships of family and kinship, of tribe and people. The Old Testament displays the special relationship, the covenant, established by God, between God and the chosen people (cf. Ex 19:4-6; Hos 2:18-23).

50. God's purpose in creation is distorted by human sin, failure and disobedience to God's will and rebellion against him. Human sin damages the relationship between God and humanity, between human beings, and between humanity and the created order. But God persists in faithfulness despite the sin and error of the people. The dynamic history of God's restoring and enriching *koinonia* with creation reaches its culmination and fulfilment in the perfect communion of a new heaven and a new earth (Rev 21).

51.   A variety of biblical images evoke the nature and quality of the relationship of God's people to God and to one another and to the created order: "the people of God" (1 Peter 2:9-10); "the flock" (Jn 10:14); "the vine" (Is 5, Jn 15); "the temple of the Lord" (1 Cor 3:16-17); "the bride of Christ" (Rev 21:2; Eph 5:25-32); "the body of Christ" (1 Cor 12:27); "the household of God" (Heb 3:1-6); "the new covenant community" (Heb 3:8-10); "the city of God – the new Jerusalem" (Is 61; Rev 21). The term *koinonia* expresses the reality to which these images refer. They evoke the depth, closeness and quality of the relationship. In the Old Testament the term *shalôm* captures something of the notion of *koinonia*.

52.   The basic verbal form from which the noun *koinonia* derives means "to have something in common", "to share", "to participate", "to have part in", "to act together" or "to be in a contractual relationship involving obligations of mutual accountability". The word *koinonia* appears in key situations, for example, the reconciliation of Paul with Peter, James and John (Gal 2:9), the collection for the poor (Rom 15:26; 2 Cor 8:4), the experience and witness of the Church (Acts 2:42-45).

53.   Through identification with the death and resurrection of Christ, by the power of the Holy Spirit, Christians enter into fellowship (*koinonia*) with God and with one another in the life and love of God: "We proclaim to you what we have seen and heard so that you may have fellowship with us. And our fellowship is with the Father and with his Son Jesus Christ" (1 Jn 1:3).

54.   The Good News is the offer to all people of the free gift of being born into the life of communion with God and thus with one another. St Paul speaks of the relationship of believers to their Lord as being "in Christ" (2 Cor 5:17) and of Christ being in the believer, through the indwelling of the Holy Spirit. Communion is the gift of God whereby God draws humanity into the orbit of the generous, divine, self giving love which flows between the persons of the Holy Trinity.

55.   It is only by virtue of God's gift of grace through Jesus Christ that deep, lasting communion is made possible; by faith and baptism, persons

participate in the mystery of Christ's death, burial and resurrection. United to Christ, through the Holy Spirit, they are thus joined to all who are "in Christ": they belong to the new communion – the new community – of the risen Lord. Because *koinonia* is also a participation in Christ crucified, it is also part of the nature of the Church and the mission of the Church to share in the sufferings and struggles of humankind.

56.   Visible and tangible signs of the new life of communion are expressed in receiving and sharing the faith of the apostles; breaking and sharing the eucharistic bread; praying with, and for, one another and for the needs of the world; serving one another in love; participating in each other's joys and sorrows; giving material aid; proclaiming and witnessing to the good news in mission; working together for justice and peace. The communion of the Church is made up of persons in community, not as independent individuals. All contribute to the flourishing of the communion.

57.   It is the will of God that the whole creation, not only the Church but all, should realize communion in Christ (Eph 1:10, 4:1-16). The Church, as communion, is instrumental to God's ultimate purpose. It exists for the glory of God to serve in obedience to the mission of Christ, the reconciliation of humankind.

58.   The divisions among the churches and the failure of their members to live in true *koinonia*, full *koinonia* with one another, affect and hinder the mission of the Church. Mission has as its ultimate goal the *koinonia* of all. The mission belongs to the essence of the nature and being of the Church as *koinonia*. This makes the restoration of unity between Christians and the renewal of their lives an urgent task.

59.   By the power of the Holy Spirit the Church lives in communion with Christ Jesus, in whom all in heaven and earth are joined in the communion of God the Holy One: this is the communion of saints. The final destiny of the Church is to be caught up in the intimate relation of Father, Son and Holy Spirit, to praise and to enjoy God for ever.

60. There remains by virtue of creation a natural bond between human beings and between humanity and creation. The new life of communion builds upon and transforms, but never wholly replaces communion given in creation, and it never within history completely overcomes the distortions of the relationship between human beings caused by sin. The old difficulties recur. The gift of communion in Christ is often restricted or only partially realized. The new life entails the constant need for repentance, mutual forgiveness and restoration. It belongs to the essence of fellowship with God that there should be continual confession of sin (1 Jn 1:7). Nonetheless, there is a genuine enjoyment of new life here and now and a confident anticipation of sharing in the fullness of communion in the life to come.

Koinonia

The notion of koinonia is being used today by many churches and in ecumenical texts as a major idea towards a common understanding of the nature and purpose of the Church. The question is being asked whether this notion is being called to bear more weight than it is able to carry.

The notion of koinonia allows separated Christians to recognize that they already share a profound degree of communion, grounded in their participation together in the life and love of God, Father, Son and Holy Spirit. The path to unity is to make that communion ever more visible. Is there a shared understanding of the language of visible communion, "fuller communion", "full communion", "perfect communion" etc. and what sense is to be made of the notions of "restricted communion", "partial communion", "impaired communion"?

As long as Christians have different ideas of what constitutes visible unity, koinonia (communion), cannot be fully realized and efforts to reach a common understanding will have to continue.

B.   Communion and Diversity

61.   Diversity in unity and unity in diversity are gifts of God to the Church. Through the Holy Spirit God bestows diverse and complementary gifts on all the faithful for the common good, for service within the community and to the world (1 Cor 12:7 and 2 Cor 9:13). No one is self-sufficient. The disciples are called to be one, while enriched by their diversities – fully united, while respectful of the diversity of persons and community groups.

62.   There is a rich diversity of Christian life and witness born out of the diversity of cultural and historical context. The Gospel has to take flesh authentically in each and every place. The faith has to be proclaimed

in language, symbols and images that engage with and are relevant to particular times and particular contexts. The communion of the Church demands the constant interplay of cultural expressions of the Gospel if the riches of the Gospel are to be appreciated for the whole people of God.

63. Authentic diversity in the life of communion must not be stifled: authentic unity must not be surrendered for illegitimate diversity. Each local church must be the place where two things are simultaneously guaranteed: the safeguarding of unity and the flourishing of a legitimate diversity. There are limits within which diversity is an enrichment and outside which it is not only unacceptable but destructive of the gift of unity. Similarly, unity, particularly when it tends to be identified with "uniformity", can be destructive of authentic diversity and thus becomes unacceptable. Through shared faith in Christ, expressed in the proclamation of the Word, celebration of the sacraments and lives of service and witness, each local Christian community participates in the life and witness of all Christian communities in all places and all times. A pastoral ministry for the service of unity and the upholding of diversity is one of the many charisms given to the Church. It helps to keep those with different gifts and perspectives mutually accountable to each other within the communion.

64. Diversity is not the same as division. Within the Church divisions (heresies, schisms, political conflicts, expressions of hatred, etc.) threaten God's gift of communion. Christians are called to work untiringly to overcome divisions, to prevent legitimate diversities from becoming causes of division, and to live a life of diversities reconciled.

Diversity

While all recognise the diversity of gifts for ministry bestowed on the Church, there is often a tendency, conscious or unconscious, to give more value to some gifts over against others. This has a destructive effect: the ordained ministry valued more highly than the gifts of lay ministries; the gifts exercised within the Church valued more highly than gifts exercised in secular contexts; oversight valued more highly than other ministries, etc.

There is a number of problems concerning the relation between Gospel and culture:

º *when one culture seeks to capture the Gospel and claims to be the one and only authentic way of celebrating the Gospel;*

º *when one culture seeks to impose its expression of the Gospel on others as the only authentic expression of the Gospel;*

º *when the Gospel is held captive within a particular cultural expression;*

º *when one culture finds it impossible to recognise the Gospel being faithfully proclaimed in another culture.*

Diversities in expression of the Gospel, in words and in actions, enrich the common life. Particular emphases today are carried in the life and witness of different churches: for example, the holiness tradition by the Methodists, the doctrine of justification by faith alone through grace by the Lutherans, the life in the Holy Spirit by the Pentecostals, the ministry of primacy in the service of unity by the Roman Catholic Church, the value of comprehensiveness by the Anglican Communion, the doctrine of deification coupled with that of "synergy" by the Orthodox, etc. How far are the different emphases conflicting positions or an expression of legitimate diversity? Does the weight placed upon the different emphases obscure the fulness of the Gospel message?

What estimate do Christians place on ecclesial and confessional identity? For some the preservation of such identity, at least for the foreseeable future, and even within a life of koinonia, is necessary for safeguarding particular truths and rich legitimate diversities that belong to a life of communion. Others understand the goal of visible communion as beyond particular ecclesial or confessional identity – a communion in which the riches safeguarded by confessional traditions are brought together in the witness and experience of a common faith and life. For others the model of "reconciled diversity" remains a compelling one. Others fear a particular model of "structural merger" in which the diversity carried by different traditions is suppressed by a rigid uniformity. Most, however, agree that an openness is required about the unity to which God calls us and that as we move by steps under the guidance of the Holy Spirit (cf. Jn 16:13) the portrait of visible unity will become clearer.

Churches understand their relation to the one, holy, catholic and apostolic Church in different ways. This has a bearing upon the way they relate to other churches and their perception of the road to visible unity.

One of the pressing ecumenical questions is how churches at this stage of the ecumenical movement can live in mutual accountability so that they can sustain one another in unity and legitimate diversity and prevent new issues from becoming causes of division within and between churches.

C.   The Church as a Communion of Local Churches

65.   From the beginning contact was maintained between local churches by collections, exchange of letters, visits and tangible expressions of solidarity (1 Cor 16; 2 Cor 8:1-9; Gal 2:9ff; etc.). From time to time, in the first centuries of the common era, local churches assembled to take counsel together. These were all ways of nurturing interdependence and maintaining communion.

66.   The communion of the Church is expressed in the communion between local churches in each of which the fullness of the Church resides. The communion of the Church embraces local churches in each place and all places at all times. Local churches are held in the communion of the Church by the one Gospel, the one baptism and the one Holy Communion, served by a common ministry. This communion is expressed in service and witness to the world.

67.   The communion of local churches is sustained by a fundamental coherence and consonance in the living elements of apostolicity and catholicity: the Scriptures, baptism, eucharist and the service of a common ministry. As "bonds of communion" these gifts serve the authentic continuity of the life of the whole Church and help to sustain the local churches in a communion of truth and love. They are given to maintain the Church in integrity as the one Church of Jesus Christ, the same yesterday, today and tomorrow. The goal of the search for full communion is realized when all the churches are able to recognize in one another the one, holy, catholic and apostolic Church in all its fullness. This full communion will be expressed on the local and universal levels through conciliar forms of life and action. In such a communion of unity and authentic diversities, churches are bound in all aspects of their life together at all levels in confessing the one faith, and engaging in worship and witness, deliberation and action.

Local Church

The term "local church" is used differently by different traditions. For some traditions the "local" church is the local congregation of believers gathered in one place to hear the Word and celebrate the sacraments. For others, "local" or "particular" church refers to the bishop with the people around the bishop, gathered to hear the Word and celebrate the sacraments. At another level, "local church" can refer to several dioceses, each with its bishop, gathered together in a synodal structure under the presidency of an archbishop, a metropolitan or a patriarch. This is the technical meaning of "local church" for the Orthodox in particular.

Each local church is united to every other in the universal Church and contains within it the fulness of what it is to be Church. In some churches local church is used of both the diocese and of the parish. There is often a mismatch between theological description of local church and how the local church is experienced by the faithful.

Churches differ according to where they perceive authority rests and how decisions are taken. For example, in some traditions authority lies primarily with the local church, in others it is focused in the worldwide college of bishops presided over by a primate, in others it lies in regional autocephalous churches, as well as on a global level through ecumenical councils presided over by a primate. This for some implies a conciliar consensus enlightened by the Holy Spirit as the only criterion of authority. In yet other traditions, authority is dispersed and the province or a regional unit is the level at which binding decisions are taken.

68.   The triune God is the source of the Church's life, its unity and its diversity. God gives to the Church all the gifts and resources needed for its life and mission. God bestows on it the apostolic faith, baptism and eucharist as means of grace to create and sustain the *koinonia*. To these are related other means which serve to keep alive and preserve the integrity of *koinonia* of the people of God.

A.   Apostolic Faith

69.   The Church is called at all times and in all places to "continue in the apostles' teaching". "The faith of the Church through the ages" is one with "the faith once for all delivered to the saints" (Jude v. 3).

70.   The apostolic faith is uniquely revealed by God in the Holy Scriptures and set forth in the Ecumenical Creeds. The Church is called upon to proclaim the same faith freshly and relevantly in each generation, in each and every place. Each church in its place is challenged in the power of the Holy Spirit to make that faith relevant and alive in its particular cultural, social, political and religious context. The apostolic faith has to be interpreted in the context of changing times and places: it must be in continuity with the original witness of the apostolic community and with the faithful explication of that witness throughout the ages.

71.   The apostolic faith does not refer to one fixed formula or to a specific phase in Christian history. The apostolic faith is confessed in worship, in life and service – in the living tradition of the Church. The faith transmitted through the living tradition of the Church is the faith evoked by the Word of God and inspired by the Holy Spirit, attested in Holy Scripture. Its content is set forth in the Ecumenical Creeds of the early Church and also testified to in other forms. It is proclaimed in many confessions of the churches. It is preached throughout the world today. This faith is nourished by and celebrated in liturgies and is manifested in service and mission of faithful Christian communities.

72. The apostolic tradition of the Church is the continuity in the permanent characteristics of the Church of the apostles: witness to the apostolic faith, proclamation and fresh interpretation of the Gospel, celebration of baptism and the Lord's Supper, the transmission of ministerial responsibilities, communion in prayer, love, joy and suffering, service to the sick and needy, communion among the local churches and sharing the gifts which the Lord has given to each.

73. Within the apostolic tradition the Ecumenical Symbol of Nicea-Constantinople (381) is a pre-eminent expression of the apostolic faith – a faith confessed everywhere, also by those who do not use this Symbol. This Creed symbolises the faith uniquely revealed in Scriptures. That same faith is expressed in the preaching, worship, sacraments, older and newer confessional statements, in the life and mission of the Church, in different cultural contexts and different ecclesial communions. The language of the Nicene-Constantinopolitan Creed, like all creeds, is conditioned by time and context. It remains the most used by Christians through the centuries and still today. Its use in confessing and praising God is both an expression of continuity through time and of communion with Christians around the world today. The non-use by some churches of this Creed should not be interpreted as a sign of their departure from the faith. In their own ways, they also confess the same apostolic faith.

74. The faith of the Church has to be lived out in active response to the challenges of every age and place. The Gospel speaks to personal and social situations, including situations of injustice, of violation of human dignity and of the degradation of creation. For example, when Christians confess that God is creator of all, this entails a life attentive to the goodness and preservation of creation. When Christians confess the one, holy, catholic and apostolic Church, this leads to working for the visible unity of the Church. Christians are called to proclaim the Gospel in word and in deed to live in their lives the message of Christ crucified and risen. Communion in faith expressed in word and life embraces both a personal and corporate dimension.

Apostolic Faith

There are churches which use creeds regularly in worship, and those which do not. They are challenged to recognize the same faith in one another's preaching, worship, sacraments, life and mission.

The apostolic faith has to be proclaimed afresh in each generation in each place. Churches differ as to what structures of conciliar communion would serve to nurture the communion in faith in changing situations.

Churches today differ concerning what are the tolerable limits to diversity in confessing the one faith. For instance, is it church-dividing:

○ *to understand the resurrection of Christ only symbolically?*

○ *to confess Christ only as one mediator among others?*

○ *to substitute the history of ancient Israel as recorded by the Old Testament with the pre-Christian history of one's own culture and people?*

○ *to understand in different ways the contribution and responsibility of the human writer in the composition of Scripture?*

○ *to consider in different ways the procession of the Holy Spirit?*

B.   Baptism

75.   In the Ecumenical Creed of Nicea-Constantinople, Christians confess "one baptism for the remission of sins". In the one baptism with water in the name of the Triune God, Father, Son and Holy Spirit, through the power of the Holy Spirit, Christians are brought into union with Christ, with each other and with the Church of every time and place. Our common baptism, which unites us to Christ in faith, is thus a basic bond of unity.

76.   Baptism is a sign of new life through Christ; the means of partici-pating in the life, death and resurrection of Jesus Christ. Baptism en-tails confession of sin, conversion of heart, pardoning, cleansing and sanctification. Baptism is the gift of the Holy Spirit and the way of incorporation into the Body of Christ: it is the sign of the Kingdom of God and of the life of the world to come. Baptism is considered to be the "ordination" of all believers.

77.   All human beings have in common their creation at God's hand, God's providential care for them, and they share in social, economic and cultural institutions which preserve human life. As persons are baptised, they "put on Christ" (Gal 3:27), they enter into the *koinonia* of Christ's Body (1 Cor 12:13), receive that share of the Holy Spirit which is the privilege of God's adopted children (Rom 8:15f), and so enjoy in anticipation that participation in the divine life which God promises and purposes for humankind (2 Peter 1:4). In the present, the solidarity of Christians with the joys and sorrows of their neighbours, their engagement in the struggle for the dignity of all who suffer, the excluded, the poor, belongs to their baptismal vocation. It is the way they are brought face to face with Christ in his identification with the victimized and outcast.

Baptism

There remain differences between some Christian traditions on:
- *the sacramental nature of baptism;*
- *the relation of baptism to faith;*
- *the action of the Holy Spirit;*
- *membership of the Church;*
- *infant baptism and baptism of those who can speak for themselves;*
- *the baptismal formula;*
- *the mode of baptism.*

The recognition of the one baptism into Christ and the fundamental bond of communion that baptism establishes raises urgent questions concerning whether there should be mutual accountability, and how it should be determined.

The recognition of the one baptism into Christ constitutes an urgent call to the churches to overcome their divisions and visibly manifest their communion in faith in all aspects of Christian life and witness.

The increasing willingness of Christians to recognise each other's baptism calls into question the practice of so-called re-baptism. Baptism is celebrated in the name of the Holy Trinity, and presupposes faith in the Holy Trinity. Accordingly, baptism performed with water in the name of, and with faith in, the Holy Trinity should be regarded by all confessions as valid and unrepeatable.

There are communities/Christians who do not celebrate the rite of baptism, yet share in the spiritual experience of life in Christ.

C.   Eucharist

78.   Baptism is very closely linked with the eucharist. Communion established in baptism is focused and brought to expression in the one

eucharist. There is a dynamic connection between baptism and eucharist. Baptismal faith is re-affirmed and grace given for the faithful living out of the Christian calling.

79.   Holy Communion is the meal where, gathered around the Lord's table, Christians receive the body and blood of Christ. It is a thanksgiving to the Father for everything accomplished in creation, redemption and sanctification; a memorial (*anamnesis*) of the death and resurrection of Christ Jesus and what was accomplished once for all on the cross; the real presence of the crucified and risen Christ giving his life for all humanity; the communion of the faithful and an anticipation and foretaste of the Kingdom to come.

80.   The confession of faith and baptism are inseparable from a life of service and witness. So too the eucharistic celebration demands reconciliation and sharing among all those regarded as brothers and sisters in the one family of God and is a constant challenge in the search for appropriate relationships in social, economic and political life (Mt 5:23ff; 1 Cor 10:14; 1 Cor 11:20-22). Because Holy Communion is the sacrament which builds up community, all kinds of injustice, racism, estrangement, and lack of freedom are radically challenged when we share in the body and blood of Christ. Through the Lord's Supper the all-renewing grace of God penetrates and restores human personality and dignity. The eucharist involves the believer in the central event of the world's history. As participants in the eucharist, therefore, we prove inconsistent if we are not actively participating in the ongoing restoration of the world's situation and the human condition. Holy Communion shows us that our behaviour is inconsistent in the face of the reconciling presence of God in human history: we are placed under continued judgement by the persistence of unjust relationships of all kinds in our society, manifold divisions on account of human pride, material interest and power politics and, above all, the obstinacy of unjustifiable confessional oppositions within the body of Christ.

Eucharist

Communion in faith and baptism finds its focus in the one eucharist. It is a matter for continuing concern among all Christians that not all Christians share together in the Holy Communion. There are those who, out of deep conviction, and on the basis of their common baptism, invite all who believe in Christ to receive, believing that eucharistic sharing is both a means of creating visible unity, and also its goal. Eucharistic hospitality is offered and received by some churches to those who are baptised and in good standing in their own churches. Others offer eucharistic hospitality in very restricted circumstances. Among still other churches, eucharistic communion is understood as the ultimate expression of agreement in faith and of a communion in life. Such an understanding would make the sharing of the Lord's Supper with those outside their own tradition an anomaly. As a result, for some churches the practice of "eucharistic hospitality" is the antithesis of the commitment to full visible unity. In spite of the range of understandings and practices there is a growing willingness to understand other positions and a shared longing to express baptismal communion in eucharistic communion as part of a life in communion.

As regards the understanding and practise of the eucharist there remains the question whether it is primarily a meal where Christians receive the body and blood of Christ, or primarily a service of thanksgiving.

Among those for whom the eucharist is primarily a service of thanksgiving, there is growing convergence concerning its sacrificial character. Remaining disagreement centres principally on the questions of how the sacrifice of Jesus Christ on Calvary is made present in the eucharistic act. A help in reconciling the different approaches has been made by the use of biblical and patristic scholarship to probe more deeply into the meaning of the biblical term anamnesis. *However, some maintain that the concept has been made to bear more weight in theological and ecumenical texts than it is capable of bearing.*

> *Churches continue to disagree on the nature and mode of the presence of Christ in the eucharist. Some important differences remain regarding the role of the Holy Spirit in the whole eucharistic celebration.*

D.   Ministry

81.   It is the vocation of the whole Church to be the servant of God's design. The Church is called at all times and in all places to serve the world.

82.   The Holy Spirit bestows gifts on every member of the Body of Christ for the building up of the fellowship of the Church and for the faithful fulfilling of the mission of Christ. All have received gifts and all are responsible. This service is offered by the whole people of God whether as individuals or as local communities or by the Church at every level of its life.

83.   As the communion of the baptised, the Church is a priesthood of the whole people of God (1 Peter 2). Jesus Christ is the unique priest of the new covenant (Heb 9:10). Christ's life was given as a sacrifice for all. Derivatively, the Church as a whole can be described as a priestly body. All members are called to offer their being as a living sacrifice and to intercede for the Church and for the world.

84.   This is true for all members of the Church, who on the basis of their common baptism, serve the world by proclaiming the Gospel, testifying to their faith through their way of life, and interceding for the salvation of the world. It is also part of their service to the world to feed the hungry, help the poor and marginalized, correct injustice, and care for the integrity of creation, together with all people of good will. In so doing, they are in harmony with the mission of the Church.

85.   From the earliest times there were those chosen by the community under the guidance of the Spirit and given specific authority and responsibility. Early in the history of the Church the need was felt for

an ordained ministry in the service of communion. Ordained ministers serve in the building up of the community, in equipping the saints, and in strengthening the Church's witness in the world. They may not dispense with the ongoing support and the encouragement of the community – on behalf of whom they are chosen, and for whom they act with the power of the Holy Spirit as representative persons. Ordained ministers have a special responsibility for the ministry of Word and sacrament. They have a ministry of pastoral care and are leaders in mission. In all of those ways they strengthen the communion in faith, life and witness of the whole people of God.

86.   There is no single pattern of conferring ministry in the New Testament. The Spirit has at different times led the Church to adapt its ministries to contextual needs; various forms of the ordained ministry have been blessed with gifts of the Spirit. The threefold ministry of bishop, presbyter and deacon was by the third century the generally accepted pattern and is still retained by many churches today, though subsequently it underwent considerable changes in its practical exercise and is still changing in most churches today.

87.   The chief responsibility of the ordained ministry is to assemble and build up the Body of Christ by proclaiming and teaching the Word of God, by celebrating baptism and the Lord's Supper and by guiding the life of the community in its worship and its mission. The whole Church and every member, served by the ordained ministry, participates in the faithful communication of the Gospel. Essential to its testimony are not merely its words, but the love of its members for one another, the quality of its service to those in need, a just and disciplined life and its fair distribution and exercise of power.

88.   The primary manifestation of apostolic succession is to be found in the apostolic tradition of the Church as a whole. In the course of history, the Church has developed several means for the handing on of apostolic truth through time, in different circumstances and cultural contexts: the scriptural canon, dogma, liturgical order, structures wider than the level of local communities. The ministry of the ordained is to

serve in a specific way the apostolic continuity of the Church as a whole. In this context, succession in ministry is a means of serving the apostolic continuity of the Church. This is focused in the act of ordination when the Church as a whole, through its ordained ministers, takes part in the act of ordaining those chosen for the ministry of the Word and sacrament.

Ministry

The location of the ministry of the ordained in, with, among or over the people of God is disputed within and among the churches.

Although convergence has taken place through multilateral and bilateral dialogues on the subject of ordained ministry there remain issues to be explored further: eucharistic presidency; the representative nature of ministry; the threefold ministry as a means to unity and an expression of unity; the nature of ordination; the ordination of only men to a ministry of word and sacrament.

There is disagreement regarding the main function of the ministry – presidency of the eucharist, preaching of the word, or both on the same level.

There is disagreement about the understanding of the representative nature of ordained ministry. For all, ministers represent the community they are called to serve. They also agree that ministers in so far as they proclaim the Word of God and administer the sacraments address the community in the name of Christ. However, they disagree about whether ordained ministers as such represent Christ.

The recognition that apostolicity and apostolic succession belong to the whole Church is an important insight for re-examining the question of apostolic continuity and its relation to ministerial continuity. (Already this has helped to make possible the establishing of communion between some churches). However, churches differ in what weight they give to the different means of maintaining apostolic continuity. There are, for example, clear differences in the churches' understanding of what the means of maintaining apostolic continuity are, how they are interrelated, to which degree they participate in the continuity promised to the Church, how apostolic continuity depends upon them (cf. Box I.A). A reason for these differences lies in the way that the churches describe the relationship between God's initiative and the response to it on the human side.

E.   Oversight: Communal, Personal and Collegial

89.   The Church as the body of Christ and the eschatological people of God is built up by the Holy Spirit through a diversity of gifts or ministries. Among these gifts a ministry of *episkopé* (oversight) serves to express and promote the visible unity of the body. Every church needs this ministry of unity in some form.

90.   The diversity of God's gifts to the Church calls for a ministry of co-ordination so that they may enrich the whole Church, its unity and mission. The gift of *episkopé* is for the service of the whole community. It is for a faithful feeding of Christ's flock, in accordance with Christ's command across the ages and in unity with Christians in different places. *Episkopé* is a requirement of the whole Church and its faithful exercise under the Gospel is of fundamental importance to its life and mission. The ministry of *episkopé* entails a mutual responsibility between those who are entrusted with oversight and the whole apostolic community of the Church. The responsibility of those called to exercise oversight cannot be fulfilled without the collaboration, support and assent of the whole community. At the same time the effective and faithful life of the community is served by a set apart ministry of leadership in mission, teaching and common life.

91.   In the course of the first centuries, communion between local congregations which had been maintained by a series of informal links such as visits, letters, collections became more and more institutionalised. Two main structures of *episkopé* emerged: personal *episkopé* and collegial *episkopé*. The purpose was to hold the local con-gregations in communion, to safeguard and hand on apostolic truth, to give mutual support, to lead in witnessing to the Gospel. All these functions are summed up in the term *episkopé*.

92.   The specific development of structures of *episkopé* varied in dif-ferent regions of the Church: this holds true both for the *episkopé* of synods and for episcopacy. The crystallization of most of the episcopal functions in the hands of one individual (*episkopos*) was much later in

some places than others. What is evident in every case, is that *episkopé* and episcopacy are in the service of maintaining continuity in apostolic truth and unity of life.

93.   At the Reformation a pluriform pattern came into being as oversight came to be exercised in a variety of ways in the churches of the Reformation. The Reformers sought to return to the apostolicity of the Church which they considered to have been marred. Pursuing this end, they saw themselves faced with the alternative of either staying within the inherited church structures or remaining faithful to the apostolicity of the Church, and thus accepted a break with the overall structure of the Church, including the ministry of universal primacy. Nevertheless, they continued to see the need for a ministry of *episkopé*, which the churches who went through Reformation ordered in different ways. There where those who exercised *episkopé* in synodal forms. Others kept or developed ministries of personal *episkopé* in various forms, according to circumstances at times closer to, at times less close to, the former medieval patterns, including for some the sign of historic episcopal succession.

Episkopé

Churches who exercise episkopé *primarily or even uniquely in synodal form and churches for whom the office of bishop is central for the exercise of* episkopé *are asked to recognize that there is a ministry of* episkopé *in both cases.*

Churches which have preserved episcopal succession are challenged to recognize both the faithful continuity with the apostolic faith as well as the apostolic content of the ordained ministry which exists in churches which have not maintained such succession and also the existence in these churches of a ministry of episkopé *in various forms. Churches without the episcopal succession, and living in faithful continuity with the apostolic faith and mission, are asked to consider that the continuity with the Church of the apostles can find expression in the successive laying on of hands by bishops and that such a sign can serve that continuity itself (cf. box of I.A (1)).*

Because of the separation of the churches there is de facto *no collegial exercise of oversight. However, the ecumenical movement is increasingly leading to a degree of shared oversight in many parts of the world. Should the sharing of oversight be increased and in what ways might it be increased?*

---

94.   A ministry of oversight implies an ordering and differentiation within the communion of the Church. Such an ordering (*taxis*) is called to reflect the quality of ordering in the divine communion of Father, Son and Holy Spirit. The Church is a communion of co-responsible persons: no function, no gift, no charisma is exercised outside or above this communion. All are related through the one Spirit in the one Body. Such an ordering which reflects divine communion cannot imply domination or subordination.

95.   Those who exercise a ministry of *episkopé* are entrusted by the Church with a specific exercise of the authority of Christ bestowed upon the Church. There is no true authority in the Church which is not empowered by the Holy Spirit for the right exercise. The model for the exercise of all oversight in the Church is Christ's own exercise of authority, as exemplified by his washing the disciples' feet, as well as Jesus' words: "I am among you as one who serves" (Lk 22:25-27; Mk 20:25-28; Mk 9:35; 10:42-35-45).

96.   The interconnectedness of the life of the Church is maintained by a ministry of *episkopé*, exercised in communal, personal and collegial ways, which sustains a life of interdependence. By synodality (communality) we mean the "walking together" of all the churches; by collegiality, the "communion" of all those who exercise oversight in them.

97.   These dimensions of oversight find expression at the local, regional and worldwide levels of the churches' life. They serve the communion of the Church maintaining its unity and diversity.

Hierarchy

Some use the word "hierarchy" to express the taxis *(order) within the Church. Their use is based on a patristic understanding of the Holy Trinity: the Father is named first as the fountainhead of all divinity, then the Son as born from the Father and then the Holy Spirit, as the one in whom God shines forth from all eternity. This hierarchy does not imply the inferiority of one of the three in the Godhead which is the perfection of communion – it is the prototype of relational life in which there is no subordination or domination and in which unity and diversity are perfectly held together. Such a view acknowledges the misuse of hierarchy throughout history.*

Others ask whether the term "hierarchy" does not imply an ontological rather than a functional understanding of the difference between ministers and lay persons, questioning at the same time the comparisons of relations between the ordained and lay with the inner Trinitarian relationships. They also reject the notion of an hierarchical ordering of ministry owing to the experience of hierarchy in an equivocal manner. In the judgment of these churches, the abuse occasioned by hierarchical structures throughout history consists primarily in the association of patterns of domination and subordination as integral to the functioning of these structures.

Insofar as the charismata cannot be exercised apart from, or over, the communion of co-responsible members, churches may wish to consider afresh the appropriateness of the language of hierarchy in the description of the ordering of ministries within the Church.

(i)   Communal (conciliar or synodal)

98. The communal (conciliar or synodal) life of the Church is grounded in the sacrament of baptism. All the baptized share a responsibility for the apostolic faith and witness of the whole Church. The

communal dimension of the Church's life refers to the involvement of the whole body of the faithful in common consultation, sometimes through representation and constitutional structures, over the wellbeing of the Church and their common involvement in the service of God's mission in the world. Communal life sustains all the baptized in a web of belonging, of mutual accountability and support. It implies unity in diversity and is expressed in one heart and one mind (Phil 2:1-2). It is the way Christians are held in unity and travel together as the one Church and the one Church is manifested in the life of each local church.

99.   The unity and communion of the Church require a ministry of discernment by the faithful. Discernment is served by the presence of the *sensus fidei* in every member of the community. The *sensus* – a kind of spiritual perception, sense, discernment (flair) – is the fruit of the indwelling of the Holy Spirit by which baptised believers are enabled to recognize what is, or is not, an authentic echo of the voice of Christ in the teaching of the community; what is, or is not, in harmony with the truth of the Gospel. The *sensus fidelium* – the expression of this *sensus fidei* by all the members – is an essential element in the discernment, reception and articulation of Christian faith.

100. All baptised members must take seriously their potential to exercise the gifts they receive from the Holy Spirit – never for their own sake alone, but for the life and mission of the whole community. All must play their part in the discernment of truth, by attentiveness to those with a special ministry of oversight and through the reception of truth. In Acts 15 the outcome of the meeting of the apostles and elders, occasioned by the problems of the local communities in their Gentile and Palestinian contexts, was through the coming together of persons chosen and appointed by the churches and "with the consent of the whole church" (Acts 15:22). In the coming together is discerned a foreshadowing of the synodality (conciliarity) of the Church. The communal life of the Church involves the coming together in council to seek and voice the mind of Christ for the Church in changing circumstances and in the face of new challenges.

(ii) Personal

101. Through the discernment of the community and under the guidance of the Holy Spirit, God calls out persons for the exercise of the ministry of oversight. Oversight is always to be exercised within and in relation to the whole Church. The Spirit who empowers those who are entrusted with oversight is the same Spirit who animates the life of all believers. On account of this, those who exercise oversight are inseparably bound to all believers. They should not be exalted over the community but always act in the spirit of the one who came not to be served but to serve.

102. Those who exercise oversight have a special duty to care for the unity, holiness, catholicity and apostolicity of the Church. In discerning vocations and in ordaining other ministries to share in the ministry of Word and sacrament, they care for the continuity of the life of the Church. In their special responsibility for maintaining the unity and continuity of the Church, they exercise discipline.

103. Primacy, wherever it exists, is an expression of the "personal" mode of ministry. It is a service of presidency to be exercised in a spirit of love and truth. Primacy is inseparable from both the collegial and communal dimensions of the Church's life. It strengthens the unity of the Church and enables it to speak with one voice.

(iii) Collegial

104. In the New Testament, it is to groups of apostles as a whole that Christ gives the commission to preach the Gospel and lead the Church. By the gathering together of those who have been entrusted with the oversight of the churches the concerns of one church are shared in the wider fellowship, and the insights of the wider Church taken back to the local church. Collegiality provides for mutual support and mutual accountability.

105. Enabling the Church to live in conformity to the mission of Christ is a continuous process involving the whole community, but within

that the gathering of those with oversight has a special role. Collegiality refers to the corporate, representative exercise in the areas of leadership, consultation, discernment, and decision-making. Collegiality entails the personal and relational nature of leadership and authority. Collegiality is at work wherever those entrusted with oversight gather, discern, speak and act as one on behalf of the whole Church. This entails leading the Church by means of the wisdom gained by corporate prayer, study and reflection, drawing on Scripture, tradition and reason – the wisdom and experience of all Church communities and of the contemporary world.

106. Sustaining collegiality involves preventing premature closure of debate, ensuring that different voices are heard, listening to expert opinion and drawing on appropriate sources of scholarship. Collegial oversight should help the Church to live in communion while the mind of Christ is being discerned. It entails making room for those of different opinions, guarding and preaching unity, even calling for restraint while giving spiritual and moral leadership. Speaking collegially does not necessarily mean agreement on every subject. It may mean reflecting back to the community the legitimate diversity that exists within the life of the Church at any given time.

Communal, Personal and Collegial

These three aspects need to be kept together. In various churches, one or another has been overemphasized at the expense of the others. In some churches, the personal dimension of the ordained ministry tends to diminish the collegial and communal dimensions. In other churches, the collegial or communal dimension takes so much importance that the ordained ministry loses its personal dimension. Each church needs to ask itself in what way its exercise of the ordained ministry has suffered in the course of history.

The language used to speak of the different dimensions of the ministry of oversight differs between churches, even between theologians in the same church and between ecumenical reports. This causes misunderstanding in conducting the debate on the ministry of oversight. The terms communal, conciliar and synodal describe the ongoing life of the whole Church and not merely particular structures and processes which serve its ongoing life.

F. Conciliarity (Communality, Synodality) and Primacy

107. Conciliarity is an essential feature of the life of the Church, grounded in the common baptism of its members (cf. 1 Peter 2). Under the guidance of the Holy Spirit, the whole Church, whether dispersed or gathered together, is conciliar. Thus conciliarity is present at all levels of the life of the Church. Conciliarity is already present in the relations which exist among the members of the smallest local communities: the relations of persons according to Gal 3:28 – "all one in Christ Jesus", excluding all divisions all forms of discrimination, domination and submission. In the local eucharistic community, conciliarity is the profound unity in love and truth between the members among themselves and with their presiding minister.

108. The interconnectedness of the life of the Church is expressed at the different levels of the Church's life, the "all in each place" linked to the "all in every place". A life of interdependence is sustained by a ministry in the service of unity. This ministry is exercised in communal, personal and collegial ways.

109. Wherever people, local communities or regional churches come together to take counsel and make important decisions, there is need for someone to summon and preside over the gathering for the sake of good order and to help the process of promoting, discerning and articulating consensus. Synods and councils of all times and in all churches demonstrate this clearly. The one who presides is always to be at the service of those among whom he/she presides for the edification of the Church of God, in love and truth. It is the duty of the president to respect the integrity of local churches, to give voice to the voiceless and to uphold unity in diversity.

110. In crucial situations synods came and come together, to discern the apostolic truth over against particular threats and dangers to the life of the Church. Their decisions were then often (though not always) recognized as the true expression of the apostolic faith. The ongoing process of reception in the life of the Church under the guidance of the Holy Spirit discerns the truth, or otherwise, of a conciliar decision.

Conciliarity and Primacy

There is still much work to be done to arrive at something like a consensus between those who do not believe that conciliarity or primacy at a world level are necessary and those who believe that full communion cannot exist without this link among all the local eucharistic communities. The lack of agreement is not simply between certain families of churches but exists within some churches. The way forward involves coming to a consensus both within each church and among the churches.

Most churches accept that a eucharist needs a president. Amongst these, there are some who would go on to say that it follows that a gathering of eucharistic communities at regional and world level similarly need a president, in the service of communion. In this perspective conciliarity implies primacy and primacy involves conciliarity.

There remain questions both within and among churches about the precise functions of a presiding minister.

111. One of the convictions which governs this whole document is that the Church is not an end in itself; it is God's gift to the world. Service belongs to the very being of the Church. Therefore, the Church of God exists only in relation to the common destiny of humanity and all creation.

112. The Church is the community of people called by God who, through the Holy Spirit, are united with Jesus Christ and sent as disciples to bear witness to God's reconciliation, healing and transformation of creation. The Church's relation to Christ entails that faith and community require discipleship in the sense of moral commitment. The integrity of the mission of the Church, therefore, is at stake in witness through proclamation and in concrete actions for justice, peace and integrity of creation. The latter will often be undertaken with those outside the community of faith. This is a defining mark of *koinonia* central for our understanding of the Church.

113. Christian discipleship is based on the life and teaching of Jesus of Nazareth testified to in Scripture. Christians are called to discipleship in response to the living Word of God by obeying God rather than human beings, repenting of sinful actions, forgiving others, and living sacrifical lives of service. The source of their passion for the transformation of the world lies in their communion with God in Jesus Christ. They believe that God, who is absolute love, mercy and justice, is working through them by the Holy Spirit. The Christian community always lives within the sphere of divine forgiveness and grace.

114. This grace calls forth and shapes the moral life of believers. Members of the Church rely on God's forgiveness and renewing grace in their faithfulness and infidelity, in their virtue and their sin. The Church does not rest on moral achievement but on justification, by grace through faith. It is on this basis that moral engagement, common action and reflection can be affirmed as intrinsic to the life and being of the Church.

115. For its part, Christian ethics relates both to the Church and to the world. It is rooted in God and shaped by the community. As such, it does not stand in isolation from the moral struggles of humankind. Christian ethics can be defined fully only in relation to both Church and world on the basis of the nature of the Church itself. Thus, complex ethical questions need serious consideration within the Church and are themselves the subject of Christian discipleship.

116. There are occasions when ethical issues challenge the integrity of the Christian community itself and make it necessary to take a corporate stance to preserve its authenticity and credibility. *Koinonia* in relation to ethics and morals means that it is in the Church that, along with the confession of the faith and the celebration of the sacraments (and as an inseparable part of these), the Gospel tradition is probed constantly for moral inspiration and insight. Situations where Christians or churches do not agree on an ethical position demand that dialogue continue in an effort to discover whether such differences can ultimately be overcome and, if not, whether they are truly church-dividing.

117. Christians and their communities are called to be accountable to each other with respect to their ethical reflections and decisions owing to the fact of their *koinonia* through faith, baptism and the Lord's Supper. This interconnectedness is manifested in their commitment to the reciprocal partnership of giving and receiving (Phil 4:15). As churches engage in mutual questioning and affirmation, they give expression to their real, but not fully realized, *koinonia*. Christians engage together in service to the world, glorifying and praising God and seeking that full *koinonia* where the life that God desires for all people and the whole creation will find fulfilment.

Faith and Ethics

The relation between faith and ethics has been seen differently during the course of Christian history. For some, the question of service to the world is an integral part of the proclamation and living of the apostolic faith itself. Others distinguish between the specifically Christian ethics (i.e. the sermon on the Mount) and the ethical code given to all human beings in which Christians also participate insofar as they are a part of humanity. For those holding the latter position, this distinction has been considered as liberating in that it enables Christians to join with others of goodwill in addressing issues of society. Yet, also in this latter group, ethical stances can be viewed to have such serious implications that they require a declaration of status confessionis.

One feature of the contemporary ecumenical situation is the frequency with which moral stances have become potentially church-dividing, both within and between churches. An increasing range of issues, including those of human sexuality, have polarized Christian communities and risk damaging or destroying the bonds of koinonia *already existing. The closer churches come to an agreement on ecclesiology, the more they are challenged to address the tolerable limits of moral diversity compatible with* koinonia. *Continual ecumenical dialogue, discernment, accountability and Christian charity are required to that end.*

VI.   FOLLOWING OUR CALLING: FROM CONVERGING UNDERSTANDINGS TO MUTUAL RECOGNITION

118. In recent years the ecumenical movement has produced many agreed statements recording converging understandings about the faith and order of the C hurch. T he m ost w ell know n of these is *Baptism, Eucharist and Ministry,* the work of the Faith and Order Commission. These converging understandings have challenged the churches to accept into their life the implications of their common affirmations. Significant proposals for steps towards greater expressions of visible unity have been enacted or are awaiting decision by the churches in virtually every part of the world. This ecumenical fact deserves affirmation.

119. Progress has shown itself concretely in the ways by which churches, according to various criteria and to varying degrees, have engaged in processes of reception and thus have advanced towards mutual recognition, or at least towards the recognition of Christian faith and life beyond their preconceived boundaries as they formally understand them to be. Some have even reached a stage of mutual recognition.

120. However, partly in response to these converging understandings there are also examples of non-reception where it has not been possible to move towards recognition. A significant symptom of this is a retrenchment often expressed in a re-confessionalism of an anti-ecumenical spirit. There are also examples of non-reception which are either the result of deeply held theological convictions or of the shortcomings of the ecumenical work itself. The churches, at all levels of their life, are all called upon to engage in the task of understanding and articulating together a common understanding of Christian identity and change, the dynamic character and the pilgrim character of the people of God.

121. The relationship between the reception of the results of theological convergence into changed lives and mutual recognition was

acknowledged in The Canberra Statement – "The Church as *Koinonia*: Gift and Calling", when it declared: "The goal of the search for full communion is realized when all the churches are able to recognize in one another the one, holy , catholic and apostolic church in its fullness" and express this in a reconciled common life.

122. Building on the convergence of earlier work, this present document is a preliminary attempt to express what the churches might now claim together about the nature and purpose of the Church, and within that perspective to state the remaining areas of difficulty and disagreement. It is our belief that if the churches are able to agree together a convergence statement on the nature and purpose of the Church, this would provide a major instrument in furthering the process of mutual recognition on the way to reconciliation.

123. Acknowledging that this present draft is only the beginning of a process in formulating a common statement on the Church, the Faith and Order Commission invites churches, commissions, theological institutes and ecumenical councils to reflect on the text in the light of the following questions (cf. also para. 7 above):

° how far can you recognize in this text an emerging convergence on the nature and purpose of the Church?

° what areas in particular do you consider need further work and what insights can you offer to progress that work?

° what other areas need to be treated in a convergence document on the nature and purpose of the Church?

° if you can recognize in this text an emerging convergence on the nature and purpose of the Church, what implications has this for your relation with other churches who may also recognize that convergence? What steps might your churches take even now towards mutual recognition?

Responses to these questions will be essential as the Faith and Order Commission seeks in the years ahead to prepare a more mature common statement on the nature and purpose of the Church.

124. It will be necessary to take these questions into serious consideration if we are to facilitate the movement from common affirmation concerning the Church, through an increasingly agreed understanding of these affirmations, to an even greater recognition of ecclesial reality in other communities than our own, and finally to the need and possibility of establishing, full, visible communion.

125. Churches will require time and creativity for reception and mutual recognition. There will need to be the acceptance that, in moving by steps and stages, developments will occur which may appear inconsistent to other churches. Yet, if the churches accept to proceed along this way, they will be a sign and a gift, in and for a fractured world, of that *koinonia* which was God's intention for the whole of humanity from the beginning of time – a *koinonia* which through the life, death and resurrection of Jesus Christ is already a reality among us, and a guarantee of that which God will fully realize at the end of history.